Original title:
Out of Orbit Odes

Copyright © 2025 Creative Arts Management OÜ
All rights reserved.

Author: Colin Leclair
ISBN HARDBACK: 978-1-80567-801-4
ISBN PAPERBACK: 978-1-80567-922-6

Shooting Star Silhouettes

In the sky, they zoom and sway,
Making wishes in a goofy way.
With twinkling tails, they prance and play,
Comets sporting a cosmic ballet.

Space squirrels tossing stardust bright,
Bonkers rockets, oh what a sight!
Chasing moonbeams, a celestial fight,
Laughter echoing through the night.

Celestial Cartography

Maps of stars with crayon lines,
Wobbly paths, like merry designs.
Planets giggling, sharing vines,
Drawing circles, oh how it shines!

Asteroids dancing in silly spins,
Gravity pulls, but laughter wins.
Venus chuckling, where the fun begins,
Charting skies, where every star grins.

The Language of Planets

Jupiter rumbles in a chuckle fit,
While Saturn wobbles, making a skit.
Mercury chats with a speed so quick,
Laughing at Earth's clumsy trick.

Neptune snickers, wrapped in blue,
While Mars throws a party for the crew.
When Pluto jokes, it's nothing new,
Stellar banter, a cosmic view.

Orbiting the Dreamscape

In dreamland's orbit, we trail and spin,
Surfing on stardust, let the giggles begin.
Wormholes twist in a playful grin,
As fantasies swirl like candy in a tin.

Unicorns soar through the galactic haze,
Stars whistle tunes that set minds ablaze.
Dancing with dreams in this whimsical maze,
Silly adventures, where laughter plays.

Fading into the Milky Way

Why did the comet cross the sky?
To catch a star for a pie in the pie!
Floating donuts in zero-gravity,
Jupiter grinning with cheeky levity.

An asteroid wearing a birthday hat,
Singing loudly, 'Hey, look where I'm at!'
Planets giggle, it's quite the spree,
While Saturn spins with glee, oh, whee!

Stardust Sentiments

A meteor shower brings such delight,
Wish upon one, what's your plight?
But be careful, they might just tease,
'We're shooting stars, now catch us, please!'

Mars, with its rust, is tickled pink,
Sipping space tea, what do you think?
With goofy satellites in a dance,
They twirl and giggle, what a chance!

Lost in Galactic Whispers

In a vacuum, a whisper was heard,
'What's the matter, do you feel blurred?'
Cosmic chuckles fill the night,
As black holes snicker, feeling quite bright!

Nebulas fluffing like cotton candy,
Hold on tight, it's really quite dandy!
Through laughter, round and round they spin,
In the great beyond, all's fun to win.

Timeless in the Cosmos

Why does time fly in the void so vast?
Because it's busy, having a blast!
Planets play hopscotch with a sigh,
While lightyears zoom by like a pie in the sky.

Galaxies whirl in a ballet so grand,
With stars doing splits, oh isn't it planned?
Cosmic giggles burst through the space,
Join the fun, let's all embrace!

Boundless Skies

Up above the clouds so high,
Where birds wear hats and squirrels fly.
A cow on a rocket, what a sight!
Mooing at stars, in the moonlight.

The sun plays hide and seek each day,
While planets dance and comets sway.
A giggling star spills cosmic beans,
Making wishes on kaleidoscope dreams.

Celestial Frequencies

Jupiter plays the tuba loud,
While Saturn wears a shiny shroud.
The asteroids tiptoe, oh so sly,
Listening to Neptune's lullaby.

Stars exchange silly glowing winks,
Filling the void with giggles and pinks.
Cosmic jokes in space abound,
Making laughter the sweetest sound.

Astral Alchemy

The moon brews tea in a golden cup,
While Martians play hopscotch, jumping up.
Wishing wells filled with starry dust,
Turning frowns into laughs, we must!

A sprinkle here, a twirl just so,
Mixing laughter in the cosmic flow.
Stars roll their eyes at silly rhymes,
Counting giggles instead of time.

Starlit Pathways

On pathways paved with sparkly light,
Space cats prance in the dead of night.
Shooting stars carry birthday cakes,
While the universe chuckles and quakes.

Nebulas paint with colors bright,
As comets chase shadows with delight.
A dance of planets, twirls and spins,
In this funny place where joy begins.

Orbiting Memories

In a spaceship made of cheese,
My thoughts float like bees.
With every nibble and bite,
I giggle into the night.

The stars wink in delight,
As I dance with pure light.
A comet whizzes right past,
I hope my snacks hold fast.

Galaxies swirl in my head,
Like jelly on bread.
I launch marshmallows with glee,
Who knew space could be so free?

A nebula's a giant puff,
My rocket's made of fluff.
Laughing with each lunar leap,
In dreams where no one sleeps.

Fragments of Infinity

A star fell right in my stew,
Now my dinner's a cosmic brew.
With space noodles that twirl and twist,
I serve the universe on a plate, can't resist.

I'm juggling planets like balloons,
Dodging Martians and cartoon raccoons.
Out here in the galactic light,
We giggle at meteors taking flight.

Time is just a rubber band,
Stretching to where I stand.
With each bounce, I snatch a dream,
And drink starlight like it's cream.

Cosmic confetti drifts down,
In my shiny space crown.
I toast to fragments so bright,
In this silly, stellar night.

Celestial Journeys

With my rocket full of snacks,
I race through cosmic cracks.
Navigating through a donut hole,
   Sipping soda, what a goal!

The moons dance with a waltz,
  Every tumble's a grand vault.
Galactic hiccups make me cheer,
As planets buzz with joyful squeer.

Gravity's just a friendly push,
   Making me spin in a lush.
  Floating high like a kite,
   In a sky that feels just right.

I crash landed on a red giant,
But the aliens were quite compliant.
They served me coffee in a cup,
And said, "You gotta lighten up!"

Beyond the Celestial Veil

I peek beyond the twinkling veil,
Where moonbeams weave a silly tale.
Whispers of stardust in the breeze,
Make my giggles float with ease.

Comets toss and tumble 'round,
While I prance on cosmic ground.
A space taco flies right by,
I take a bite, oh me, oh my!

Shooting stars barter wishes,
For slices of floaty, giggly dishes.
Nebulas puff with colored air,
As we play hopscotch with flair.

With friends in every constellation,
We celebrate our odd creation.
Beyond the veil, with laughter so sweet,
It's a universe of fun, oh what a treat!

The Silence Between Stars

In the void where laughter floats,
Galaxies giggle, tickling comets' throats.
Whispers of suns, a cosmic prank,
As black holes burp, not much to thank.

Asteroids skip like stones on waves,
While Venus winks from her sultry caves.
The Milky Way tosses jokes on high,
Spinning tales in the ink of the sky.

Chronicles of the Cosmos

Once there was a moon, so very cheeky,
Trotting round Earth, feeling quite sneaky.
Stars wrote notes in a secret code,
As Martians chuckled on their dusty road.

A rogue planet wandered, lost and bewildered,
While Saturn's rings danced, never hindered.
The universe laughed, a mischievous jest,
Creating pranks, it's simply the best!

Ephemeral Stardust

Fleeting sparkles on cosmic streams,
Dust bunnies in space, or so it seems.
Nebulas pouted, all puffed and bright,
While quasar giggles lit up the night.

Shooting stars dart with playful glee,
Do they wish for tacos? Oh, let it be!
In this realm of whimsy, such fun we find,
Where the absurd dances, and logic's blind.

Dance of the Planets

Planets twirl in a merry tune,
Jupiter trips, but won't see the moon.
Mars does the limbo, low and slow,
While Mercury zips with a flashy glow.

Earth joins in with a cheeky twist,
Around the sun, how can we resist?
So grab a partner, spin and glide,
In this cosmic gala, let joy reside!

Celestial Currents

In the cosmos, a comet sneezed,
Asteroids danced, and giggled, pleased.
Wormholes pull socks in a spin,
While aliens chuckle at what's within.

Planets play tag, it's quite the race,
Saturn rings in his own slow space.
Mars throws confetti, a red-pink flair,
While Pluto pouts, 'That's not fair!'

Songs of the Floating World

Singing stars hum in gleeful tones,
While moons juggle cheese and comets throw stones.
A spaceship with hiccups drifts by,
Leaving stardust trails in the sky.

Floating fish in nebula waves,
Shout, 'We're lost, but we feel brave!'
Gravity giggles at silly pranks,
While the sun gives funky dance flanks.

Navigating Starlit Paths

Lost in space with a map of pizza,
A guide who's an owl with a slice of feta.
We hit a black hole and twirl about,
While lightsabers flicker, giggling out loud.

Asteroids shout, 'Hey, watch your step!'
As meteors pee-pee dance, oh, what a rep!
Galaxies cheer, making ruckus so loud,
A party in space, we feel so proud.

The Expanse of Longing

Stars yearn for hugs, but it's hard to reach,
They wave across space, in a radiant speech.
Shooting stars send wishes with flair,
While black holes wonder, 'Who's really there?'

In the quiet of space, a giggle erupts,
As planets collide, and all joy erupts.
Comets chase dreams on a trampoline,
A universe filled with silly routine.

Journey Through Stardust

In a rocket made of cheese,
We fly past saucer trees.
Jupiter winks, a cosmic tease,
Watch out for those comet fleas!

Mars is hosting a dance tonight,
With aliens dressed in pastel light.
We're lost in space, what a sight!
Who knew flight would feel so right?

Asteroids throwing a wild bash,
With moon rocks rolling in a flash.
Gravity's gone—oh what a clash!
Space cats purring; they're here to splash!

Let's grab some stars, they're on sale,
Shooting past, a glowing trail.
With laughter loud, we set our sail,
To disco worlds, we will not fail!

Cosmic Kaleidoscope

Galaxies swirl like cotton candy,
Meteors falling, oh so dandy.
Aliens giggle, not too handy,
Trading spacerock for a brandy.

Planets spin like tops in flight,
Saturn dances, rings so bright.
Uranus jokes, 'I'm out of sight!'
While Venus sticks to fashion's plight.

Stars are blinking, winking cheeky,
Celestial bodies getting freaky.
A cosmic joke that feels quite sneaky,
This universe is far from meeky!

In this vast, starry art gallery,
Each twinkle tells a tale quite merry.
Hold on tight, let's go contrary,
Into a world where joy is ordinary!

Observing the Unseen

Peering through a telescope wide,
I saw a comet take a slide.
It tripped and fell, oh how it cried,
While stars above just laughed and pried.

Hidden worlds beneath the haze,
Life forms playing mindless games.
A giant worm with neon flames,
Shouting, 'Catch me!' as it claims.

Black holes beckon, 'Come take a dive!'
But spinning too fast, we won't survive.
They chuckle, 'Only the brave thrive!'
In this vacuum, our hopes arrive.

Ghostly satellites toast with cheer,
Floating shadows—what do we fear?
Invisible friends, drawing near,
In cosmic limbo, nothing clear!

Celestial Rhythms

The sun beats down, a funky tune,
Planets clap, we start to swoon.
Dancing moons in a lively croon,
While comets join in—what a boon!

Galactic disco, space boots on,
Asteroids groove, till the break of dawn.
Gravity defies, our worries gone,
With every beat, we feel reborn.

Stars catch light and sway with glee,
A cosmic party, wild and free.
Satellites spinning, what jubilee!
Come join our dance, you'll see, you'll see!

In this rhythm, we float along,
Anonymous beats, where we belong.
With each rotation, a joyful song,
In this tapestry, we can't go wrong!

Nocturne of the Nebulae

Twinkling stars with sleepy grins,
Dreaming of cosmic jellyfin.
Asteroids dance in fancy shoes,
While comets gossip, sharing news.

The Milky Way plays hide and seek,
While black holes giggle, oh so meek.
Planets spin in a waltz divine,
Drifting through space, sipping moonshine.

Galactic squirrels eat stardust pie,
As meteors zoom past with a sigh.
What a sight, such a cosmic show,
Laughing with stars, going with the flow.

Cosmic Tides

Waves of stardust crash and play,
Alien frogs hop in Milky Way.
Saturn's rings keep losing track,
Of all the space snacks kept in back.

Shooting stars, like fireflies bright,
Wishing for snacks and silly fights.
Planets hum a snazzy tune,
While meteor showers get a boon.

Galaxies swirl like they're on skates,
Flaunting their spins and fancy plates.
Cosmic tides wash dreams ashore,
As laughter echoes forevermore.

Beyond the Event Horizon

What lies beyond that dark veil,
Where space and time begin to flail?
Wormhole winks with a cheeky grin,
As lounge chairs float in a cosmic din.

Time-travelers wear goofy hats,
While floating by a red giant's spats.
They toast with fizz from stellar springs,
As quasars laugh at all these things.

Gravity pulls pranks on the sly,
As planets wink and the comets fly.
A dance of light, a jolly spree,
In the place where fun meets zero-G.

Dawn of the Galaxy

Morning breaks in a burst of spark,
Where aliens race in a galactic park.
Pancakes flip on a sunbeam grill,
While star-naps end with a joyful thrill.

Looks like the sun forgot his hat,
The space cows giggle, oh imagine that!
Nebulas puff with a colorful sigh,
As cosmic crickets chirp nearby.

Spaceships zoom to the rhythm of cheer,
As rockets blast off with a delighted jeer.
In this realm where giggles sprout,
The galaxy wakes, and fun's what it's about.

Echoes of Celestial Whispers

The stars all giggle in the night,
Chasing comets with all their might.
Planets twirl in a silly dance,
While asteroids refuse to take a chance.

Neptune sneezed, oh what a blast,
Mars just laughed and fell down fast.
With each backflip, the Milky Way,
Teases black holes to join the play.

Saturn's rings are hula hoops,
While aliens share their noodle soups.
Galaxies wink and share old jokes,
Among the cosmic laughing folks.

In this space of joy and cheer,
Even rockets ask for a beer.
Stardust tickles with a soft embrace,
And silly laughter fills the space.

A Cosmic Embrace

Two meteors met and shared a kiss,
They giggled at a space-time miss.
The sun waved with a flaming hand,
As they danced across the twinkling land.

Jupiter pulls pranks on his moons,
Playing hide and seek with tune-filled tunes.
Mercury zooms past with a sassy wink,
While the black holes just sit and think.

A cosmic pillow fight ignites,
With starlight fluff and giggly lights.
Nebulas burst with colorful glee,
Painting smiles on the galactic sea.

Astrophysicists scratch their heads,
Wondering why stardust beds.
In the vastness, they can feel the grace,
Of a universe bursting with silly face.

Uncharted Nebulae

In a cloud of colors, jokes unfold,
As galaxies gather, brave and bold.
A spaceship shot out silly confetti,
Leaving trails of laughter, wild and jetty.

Stars wear hats made of space debris,
Joking about who's lost in the spree.
An astronaut trips on a comical dream,
Floating away like a lost ice cream.

Quasars wink, pulling pranks in sight,
While space whales sing through the night.
The vacuum hums a playful tune,
As planets glide under the playful moon.

In this wild and wacky array,
Even the asteroids want to play.
Navigating humor with a twist,
In these nebulous laughs, we coexist.

Ethereal Horizons

Beyond the stars, where laughter grows,
Cosmic clowns juggle space-time flows.
Galactic giggles echo, oh so bright,
As comets skate on the edge of night.

The universe plays a game of charades,
With black holes hiding in colorful shades.
Each supernova bursts with a cheer,
As constellations crack jokes, loud and clear.

Falling stars make wishes, but don't you see?
They're just hoping for a cup of tea.
Celestial bodies share cosmic puns,
While Saturn's rings spin around just for fun.

In this realm of ethereal light,
Every cosmic corner is sheer delight.
From asteroids to quasars, with joy we soar,
In laughter's embrace, who could ask for more?

Eclipsed Dreams

In the sky, a banana moon,
Swallowed whole by a silly tune.
Stars backed away, unsure of the scene,
Counting the laughs in a cosmic routine.

Aliens dance with two left feet,
Sipping on stardust, a tasty treat.
Wormholes twist in a playful way,
Who knew space could have such sway?

Planets spin like plates on a stick,
One fell down, it made quite a trick.
Galaxies giggle in the vastness,
Floating around in a cosmic mess.

Asteroids laughing, they honk as they ride,
Joyful chaos, there's no need to hide.
In this cosmic jest, dreams take flight,
Chasing the stars in the deep of night.

Cosmic Serenade

A comet plays a saxophone tune,
While UFOs tap dance under the moon.
Saturn's rings are just disco lights,
With Martians grooving on wild moonlit nights.

Mercury mischief, quick on his toes,
Slips on a comet, and oh! How it goes.
Planets chime in with bell-like glee,
Twinkling along in cosmic harmony.

Black holes swirl in a haphazard waltz,
Missing their cue, oh what a fault!
Laughing at space in a jolly parade,
Every planet throwing confetti displayed.

Galactic giggles fill up the vast,
Time slips away, but the fun will last.
In this mad dance of the great unknown,
Joy is the language, and love is the tone.

Stardust Echoes

Stars whisper secrets in silver-light,
While asteroids argue about who's right.
Shooting stars compete in a silly race,
Landing right back in their cosmic place.

In the Milky Way, hiccups abound,
Black holes grinning, swirling around.
The sun wears shades with laughter so bright,
As planets gossip in the deep of night.

Cosmic crabs scuttle on lunar sands,
Offering samples of dreamlike plans.
They chuckle as meteors make a splash,
Leaving trails that twinkle, and then they dash.

With each stardust echo, joy takes flight,
Weaving through galaxies, pure delight.
In this universe where laughter's the aim,
We're all just players in a grand cosmic game.

Nebula's Lament

A nebula sighs, plush clouds of pink,
Her jovial fluff starts to boldly blink.
Stars rolled their eyes at her colorful cry,
Why so dramatic? It's only the sky!

Quasars giggle at her overly soft,
Spinning through galaxies, feeling quite swathed.
"Why so gloomy, dear?" they tease and they jest,
"Could it be you're feeling a bit under-dressed?"

Cosmic critters gather, a party's in store,
Lighting up dark with a fabulous lore.
In a tangle of light, they dance and delight,
Transforming her blues into laughter so bright.

So nebulae sparkle, forgotten the woe,
Embracing the chaos of stardust's glow.
In this playful realm, all worries take flight,
Where the universe bumbles, feels perfectly right.

Aurora of the Unseen

The stars have jokes, but we can't hear,
They twinkle with laughter, what a cheer!
Planets spin tales, in cosmic talks,
While left-over asteroids jog like flocks.

Black holes hide secrets, they never share,
Swallowing light, they giggle with flair.
Comets with tails, like dogs running wild,
Zoom past the moon, just a playful child.

Stardust throws parties on distant shores,
Each grain a whisper of galactic roars.
Nebulas dance in their colorful dress,
While shooting stars laugh at our earthbound stress.

So when you look up, don't just admire,
Join in the fun, fuel your cosmic fire!
The universe chuckles, a vibrant embrace,
A funny ballet in the vastness of space.

Notes from the Ether

A message from Mars, in a bottle adrift,
Cracked space humor, like a cosmic gift.
Jupiter's storms, they crack jokes with ease,
While Saturn's rings giggle in the breeze.

A satellite spins, with a grin on its face,
Broadcasting puns through this weightless place.
Elongated beings dance in zero-G,
Wobbling like jelly, how funny to see!

Uranus jokes, 'I'm the butt of it all,'
While Mercury zips, never late for a call.
Venus throws shade, all lush and confused,
Yet finds it amusing, like it's all just a ruse.

In the grand cosmic play, each world takes a part,
Their laughter rings true, pure celestial art.
So tune in your heart to the ether's good vibes,
And join in the chuckles the starlight prescribes.

Celestial Reflections

In mirrors of space, we catch funny sights,
Where the moons hold debates, and the stars spark fights.
A quasar grins wide, with a radiant gleam,
While space-tigers giggle in a photon dream.

Zany constellations roll over at night,
Big Dipper and friends, what a comical sight!
Cosmic tumbleweeds float through the air,
While lazy asteroids lounge without a care.

A space whale swims through the galaxy wide,
Telling tall tales of the tide's cosmic ride.
The Milky Way laughs with a twinkling jest,
While a sunbeam whispers, "You're simply the best!"

So let your eyes wander among starry beams,
Join in the laughter, it's all in your dreams.
In the cosmic mirror, we're quite the odd lot,
Reflecting the funny, and giving it thought.

Beyond the Event Horizon

What lies past the veil of a black hole's fold?
A comedy club, or so I've been told.
Black holes tell tales, but you can't take them in,
Too busy just swirling, round in a spin.

A theory of laughter floats 'round in the dark,
Where jokes are born bright and humor leaves a mark.
Wormholes connect punchlines, wrapped tight in their loops,
And space-faring gnomes share their inside scoops.

On gravitational waves, a giggle takes flight,
Riding the tides of the vastness at night.
Neutron stars pulsing with a rhythm that rocks,
Crack jokes like clockwork, with cosmic tick-tocks.

So reach for the stars, embrace the delight,
For the world of the cosmos is fanciful, bright!
In the endless expanse, where punchlines collide,
Let hilarity reign, with the universe as guide.

The Cosmic Dance

In spacesuits we waltz with stars,
Twinkling with laughter, past Mars.
The Milky Way twirls in delight,
Spinning the universe, oh what a sight!

With comets as partners, we glide,
Bouncing off moons, we can't hide.
Space socks on, we slide with glee,
This galactic groove sets us free!

Planets chuckle, they can't resist,
In this cosmic dance, we coexist.
Orbiting laughter, a jovial spree,
As gravity tickles, we shout, "Whee!"

In the cosmos, we're all a bit odd,
So let's two-step with our weirdness, applaud!
From Nebulae to quarks, we prance,
Every starlight flicker, a chance to dance!

Stellar Reverberations

Echoes of laughter refound,
As stars sing together, profound.
A black hole burps, causing a roar,
Supernovae giggle, forevermore.

The asteroids joke in their rings,
While Saturn boasts of bling-bling.
Nebulas swirl, a cosmic ballet,
Creating confetti of night and day.

Radiowaves bounce, tickling our ears,
As aliens dance, shedding their fears.
The universe hums a silly tune,
Inviting all life to join very soon.

With pulsars pulsing, we keep the beat,
Even galaxies wobble on their feet.
Cosmic chuckles through the void reign,
In this stellar symphony, joy is our gain!

Celestial Melodies

Singing stars with voices so bright,
Compose a tune in the cool night.
Shooting stars shimmy, oh what fun,
As meteors dance, one by one.

The moon's a DJ, spinning the night,
With cosmic beats, it feels just right.
Planets clap hands, while comets swoon,
This galactic party starts very soon.

Saturn's rings twang like a guitar,
While Jupiter laughs and plays bizarre.
With every pulse, a cosmic laugh,
Creating a melody, our own autograph.

Let's serenade with the Milky Way,
As stardust whispers, "Join our play."
In this vast theater, we twirl and sway,
Singing together, hip-hip-hooray!

Exploring Dark Matter

We seek what's hidden, a sneaky affair,
In shadows and whispers, wink and stare.
Dark matter giggles, it knows we're near,
With hints around corners, alludes to fear.

Wormholes seem wobbly, what a surprise,
We snicker at theories that don't tell lies.
Scientists scratching their heads in confusion,
As we discover space's unique illusion.

Black holes are moody, they chomp quite a bit,
Eating up stars with a sulky fit.
But we've got jokes to lighten the gloom,
As space-time chuckles, "Make room, make room!"

Exploring the void, we're odd, it's true,
Together we search, just me and you.
In this cosmic quest, let's find the fun,
With dark matter's laughter, we've only begun!

Voices from the Cosmos

In space where the stars do twine,
Aliens sing in a wobbly line.
Planets giggle, they bounce around,
As comets fart with a whooshy sound.

Saturn tosses its rings in glee,
While Mars claims it's got the best tea.
Neptune laughs, says it's quite a joke,
When Earth spills coffee—oh, the smoke!

Celestial Drift

A spaceship drifts with a silly glide,
While the stars laugh and take a ride.
They trade jokes with meteor showers,
While Saturn blooms its strange flower.

Jupiter belches a cosmic burp,
While tiny asteroids start to chirp.
Galaxies dance in a messy spin,
As black holes giggle, 'Let the fun begin!'

Spirals of Stardust

Stardust puffs like fluffy clouds,
While supernovas gather crowds.
They toss sparkles, play peek-a-boo,
And laugh as they stick like goo.

Cosmic critters run around fast,
Chasing light, not thinking of the past.
They tumble through void, it's sheer delight,
In the endless dance of the night!

Wandering Light

Light beams wander, taking their stroll,
Making shadows, they play the whole.
Tickling moons with a gentle sway,
While giggling stars come out to play.

A nebula hums a silly tune,
While planets moonwalk under the moon.
Constellations wink, oh what a sight,
As space itself joins in the light!

Luminous Shadows

In the dark, a glow does creep,
Moonbeams play, while planets sleep.
Stars above with a twinkle bright,
Whisper jokes in the cool, clear night.

Asteroids roller-skate 'round the sun,
Laughing as they spin and run.
Gravity's tug is a silly tease,
Caught in an orbit of cosmic freeze.

Comets flash by with tails of light,
Winking at black holes, what a sight!
Galaxies dance, like people in hats,
With spacetime bends, we all have chats.

Nebulas puff, like smoke rings blown,
Creating shapes that we've never known.
A stellar joke, in the cosmic sea,
Who knew space could be so free?

Aether's Ballet

In a swirl of stars that jig and jive,
Planets spin as if they're alive.
A ballerina comet takes the stage,
Twisting through space, a galactic rage.

Satellites giggle in loops and twirls,
Dancing with light from their orbital swirls.
Astrological partners, quite the sight,
Holding hands in the velvet night.

A black hole hiccups, a comical feat,
Pulling in matter with a gravitational greet.
While moons do a tango, huge and round,
In this aether ballet, joy is found.

Stars bow down, take a clumsy fall,
Hitchhiking meteors join the ball.
When the curtain falls, applause will boom,
For the cosmos' fun-filled dance in bloom!

Dancing with the Void

In the void, there's a quirky tune,
Dancing shadows chasing the moon.
Stars lock arms, a celestial hug,
While Saturn twirls in a playful tug.

Supernova bursts with a cheerful grin,
Sprinkling stardust, let the fun begin.
Whirling galaxies in a waltz divine,
Funny gravity, it bends the line.

Quasars giggle with bizarre delight,
Sending signals, oh what a night!
Black holes whisper secrets so sly,
As we dance around, oh my oh my!

The universe spins in wild array,
Cosmic jokes in a grand ballet.
Together we laugh with the things we find,
In this void, our joy's unconfined.

Interstellar Emotions

In space, emotions play hide and seek,
Stars are grumpy, yet comets peek.
Planets blush when they twirl around,
While the moon, full of pride, makes no sound.

Meteor showers screen love notes true,
Though those wishing rocks don't always come through.
Shooting stars, with a wink and a smile,
Think they're the cool kids — just for a while.

Cosmic giggles explode in delight,
When asteroids bicker; oh, what a fight!
But when the dust settles, they hug it out,
In the vastness of space, there's no room for doubt.

So we drift through emotions, light years apart,
With laughter echoing right from the heart.
In the grand scheme of stars and fate,
It's funny how love makes us all relate.

Lunar Lullabies

The moon sings sweetly, a silver tune,
Dreams float gently, like dandelion fluff.
Stars giggle softly, in the night sky's room,
Whispering secrets, in a cosmic puff.

Lunar cows jump over the milky waves,
Dancing in moonlight, how silly they seem.
Planets play tag, oh, the mess that it saves,
Comets burst laughing, like popcorn in steam.

Space bears in pajamas, they snore with delight,
Winking at asteroids, all in the fray.
Galaxies twirl in a vibrant ballet,
While Martian mimes mime in pure black and white.

Cosmic pies floating, with sprinkles and cheer,
Chasing the stars, they wobble with glee.
Neighbors pitch in, sharing laughter and beer,
Who knew that stardust could tickle like me!

The Space Between Hearts

A heartbeat echoes, across the vast night,
With comets colliding like kisses so bold.
Love's rocket ships soar, with an engine of flight,
Through galaxies swelling, with stories untold.

Celestial giggles tickle the silence,
While aliens wink from their rainbow-hued scouts.
Cupid shoots arrows, with utmost defiance,
Finding lost lovers in black holes and shouts.

Hearts made of stardust, they bounce and they blend,
Like planets that hug in a space-time embrace.
Friendships in orbit, they twist and they bend,
Hitchhikers smiling, enjoying the race.

Floating on wishes and big cosmic dreams,
With rockets of laughter, we're never alone.
The universe hums, or so it still seems,
In the heart of the void, we've made it our home.

A Journey Through Starlit Skies

We packed up our dreams, took off on a whim,
With snacks made of meteor and juice made of stars.
Zooming through cosmos on a whimsy-trimmed rim,
While planets waved hello, not caring for cars.

Riding on comet tails, we giggled and twirled,
Spinach-flavored moon pies brought smiles to our face.
Galactic mischief, such a wacky world,
As we tumbled and laughed, in an astral race.

Chasing the sunbeams, we danced in the glow,
While shooting stars pranced like a carnival ride.
Upside-down planets, oh what a show,
With space llamas joined in, our laughter our guide.

With each funky orbit, oh, what a surprise,
We found silly wonders in each cosmic bend.
Through stardust adventures, beneath giggly skies,
Our joy in this journey will never quite end.

The Tides of Cosmic Yearning

Waves of stardust crash on shores of delight,
Wish upon ripples where dreams gently play.
The tide pulls and giggles beneath the bright light,
As planets conspire to make mischief all day.

Galaxies sway, like lovers who croon,
With arms made of meteors, twinkling in dance.
Cosmic seashells whisper a melodic tune,
Seducing the stars into odd circumstance.

Jellyfish shimmer in rainbow-streaked streams,
While aliens build castles of chocolate and glee.
Sirens of Saturn sing wild lullabies,
Welcoming travelers from moons we can't see.

The shores of the cosmos, they sparkle and shine,
With laughter and joy, they beckon us near.
A journey of fun, where absurdity's fine,
The tides of our dreams swirl in space without fear.

Comet's Canvas

A comet dashed across the night,
Its tail a brush of pure delight.
It painted stars with silly grace,
Made the moon laugh, a glowing face.

Planets watched with bulging eyes,
As space debris danced in the skies.
Asteroids giggled in a pack,
While meteorites tried to keep track.

Shooting stars took selfies bold,
While rocket ships spun tales untold.
The Milky Way joined in the dance,
As space went wild, gave chaos a chance.

So wave your hands, give a cheer,
For cosmic silliness shines so clear.
In this vastness, joy takes flight,
With comets crafting art at night.

Nebula's Song

In the heart of swirling hues,
A nebula sings its jolly blues.
With clouds that wiggle and do the twist,
In cosmic parties, they can't resist.

Stars pop out like party balloons,
While comets groove to funky tunes.
Quasars blink in a playful tease,
As cosmic winds play the cosmic keys.

Supernova bursts with a giggle,
As dust clouds start to jiggle and wiggle.
Gravitational pulls join the fun,
In this starry dance, we're all one.

Laughter echoes through black holes,
As space-time stretches to meet our souls.
In this concert of light and cheer,
The universe laughs, come lend an ear!

Galactic Reflections

In the mirror of space, stars wink bright,
Reflecting giggles in the night.
Galaxies swirl with whimsical flair,
Creating a cosmic show beyond compare.

Planets peer from their cozy beds,
With pillows made of starry heads.
Saturn's rings twirl, what a sight,
As it jests with Jupiter in delight.

Starlight whispers secrets and puns,
As black holes say they're the only ones!
Cosmic humor in every turn,
Lighting up the night, we all yearn.

So let's toast with asteroid wine,
To celestial dreams that intertwine.
In the grand reflections of our fate,
The universe chuckles, isn't it great?

Dreamscapes in the Sky

Floating dreams on stellar streams,
Clouds of cotton candy and marshmallow beams.
Cosmic sheep jump over the moon,
As space giggles a silly tune.

UFOs play hopscotch with stars,
While planets trade their cosmic cars.
Galactic kites drift gently high,
In a playful breeze, oh my, oh my!

Asteroids race on a slippery track,
While comets say, 'You can't catch back!'
In spacescapes, laughter's a blast,
As we dream our futures, bright and vast.

So close your eyes and take the ride,
On the magic carpet of the sky wide.
With spacespun giggles, forever carefree,
Embrace the dreamscape, come dance with me!

Chasing Comets

With tails of ice and dust, they zoom,
A cosmic race through the night's gloom.
I tripped on my laces, fell on the ground,
While comets just giggled, spinning around.

I waved hello, they just flew by,
Shooting stars that make me sigh.
I need a rocket, or maybe a boat,
To sail on the sky, like a cosmic float.

They dart and dash, with blurs of light,
I bounce like a ball, what a funny sight!
Gravity laughs, keeping me still,
While comets just grin, with speed and thrill.

In my backyard, I try to leap,
While galaxies wink where secrets sleep.
Each blink brings dreams of space-age fun,
As I chase those comets, one by one.

Dreams Beyond the Celestial Sphere.

I dreamt I flew on a marshmallow cloud,
With an alien DJ, spinning loud.
We danced on rings of Saturn's grace,
While planets joined in, a wild space race.

I asked for fries from a shooting star,
But it served me salad from afar.
With vinaigrette from a comet's tail,
I dined in style, on a cosmic trail.

A moonbeam winked, said, "Let's play!"
We played hide and seek, in a stellar ballet.
I chased my dreams through a purple haze,
Laughing with asteroids in a quirky daze.

In this wacky world of delights so bright,
Where space suits shimmer with glittery light,
I twirled through constellations, just for fun,
Dreams beyond the sphere, never to shun.

Celestial Reveries

A star fell down to join my tea,
It said, "I'm lonely, come wild with me!"
We spun tales of planets made of cheese,
And laughed with comets, swaying in the breeze.

In cosmic cafes, we sip on air,
With astronauts juggling, without a care.
The moons all chuckle at misfit dreams,
As we feast on stardust, or so it seems.

Floating past the Milky Way's swirl,
I offered a planet to my favorite girl.
She laughed and said, "No rocks, just ice!"
In the kitchen of space, we made it nice.

From nebulae gardens, we pick bright blooms,
Creating bouquets in our starry rooms.
The laughter echoes, as we play together,
In celestial reveries, light as a feather.

Gravity's Whisper

Gravity whispered, "You're such a clown,"
As I floated up, then plopped right down.
With rockets strapped to my old rubber boots,
I tumbled and giggled, while chasing my roots.

The planets rolled over, shaking their rings,
They laughed till they sparked with all of their flings.
I tried to dance in a pearly swirl,
But tripped on stardust, oh what a whirl!

"Let's have a party," cried the moons so bright,
As asteroids boogied in sheer delight.
With meteor showers making a show,
We laughed till we cried in a cosmic flow.

In the night sky, our giggles reside,
While planets and comets all gently glide.
Gravity's whispers keep us in tune,
As we twirl and spin like a cartoon balloon.

Whims of the Universe

The stars were having a waltz one night,
They tripped over comets, oh what a sight!
Planets played tag, each making a dash,
While black holes giggled, causing a crash.

Jupiter's storm was a carnival fun,
It tossed little moons like popcorn in sun.
Mars wore a wig made of dust and good cheer,
While Saturn spun rings, but lost one, oh dear!

Neptune, the prankster, threw ice on the sun,
Said, 'Come catch me, if you think you can run!'
Asteroids danced in a cosmic parade,
While the Milky Way winked, 'Aren't we all played?'

The universe chuckled, it's full of such quirks,
With cosmic shenanigans and humorous perks.
So next time you gaze up and see that vast dome,
Remember, the stars are not all that alone!

Timekeepers of the Cosmos

Two clocks in space twirled their hands,
One said it's noon as the other just stands.
They bickered and squabbled o'er timezones unknown,
While galaxies giggled at their little drone.

Black holes pouted, 'It's not fair you know,
Time skips us by, like a depressed old show!'
While quasars laughed, with their light-speed glow,
'At least you're still here, just go with the flow!'

Wormholes showed up wearing tops and a bow,
'We're here for a party! Come on, let's go!'
But timekeepers grinned, with their hands all a-twirl,
As seconds and minutes began to unfurl.

The cosmos shrugged, 'Let's just have some fun,'
'Who cares about time when you're dancing with sun?'
So twirl and spin, dear timekeepers and jest,
In the grand cosmic plan, you're just part of the jest!

Ethereal Driftwood

Floating through space, driftwood arrives,
With tales of the stars and where laughter thrives.
Each fragment a memory, a giggle or sigh,
In the vastness of cosmos, who really knows why?

A log from a comet with bark made of light,
Told stories of black holes that popped into night.
While stardust skated on rings made of dreams,
And wormholes were laughing, bursting at seams.

The driftwood saw planets that danced on a whim,
And said, 'Join in the fun, you can't be so grim!'
As supernovae showered surprise sparkles bright,
The wood chuckled softly, 'What a cosmic delight!'

So if you see driftwood afloat in the void,
Remember its laughter, the joy it enjoyed.
For in this great universe, wild and untamed,
Even driftwood finds ways to be humorously framed!

Orbiting the Infinite

Two asteroids spun in a game of charades,
While meteors giggled, tossing silly grenades.
The sun played a tune, oh what a ruckus!
While planets rolled by, all perplexed and fussed.

Galaxies swirled, as if stuck in a trance,
While moons showed off moves, taking a chance.
Uranus winked back, with a cheeky glint,
'Have you seen my rings? I'm still on a sprint!'

Little comets zoomed with a spark and a squeal,
Their tails all a-wag, showing out their zeal.
The universe chuckled, how odd it all seemed,
In this cosmic playground, where laughter redeemed.

So orbit with glee, let your heart wildly spin,
In the dance of the stars, let the joy seep in!
For in this vast cosmos, so funny and bright,
Each movement a giggle, a wondrous delight!

Cosmic Heartstrings

In a galaxy so wide, we twirl,
With space dust tangled in a whirl.
Martians dance on pogo sticks,
While shooting stars play pranks and tricks.

Aliens with hats, they jive and swing,
Telling tales of cosmic bling.
With zero gravity, we float about,
Laughing till the kind comets shout.

A neutron star dressed as a clown,
Sends ripples through this cosmic town.
Saturn's rings are all a-glow,
As we laugh and twirl in the stardust flow.

Let's ride these beams of pure delight,
And toast to all that is insight.
In this universe of giggles and grins,
We celebrate—where joy begins!

The Astral Pulse

There's a beat in the cosmos, a funny sound,
A comet's chuckle flies all around.
Planets roll with belly laughs,
As quasars share their silly halves.

Uranus gave a cheeky wink,
While Venus pondered—did I just blink?
Neptune's got the best dad jokes,
And Mars is filled with quirky blokes.

Each star's a giggle, each moon a tease,
Dust bunnies dance in the cosmic breeze.
With laughter swirling through the void,
Interstellar fun that can't be destroyed.

So let's groove to the astral beat,
With cosmic kicks that can't be beat.
The universe spins, a merry spree,
In this vast playground, come jump with me!

Transcendence of the Skies

In the fabric of space, unraveling fun,
A celestial party is just begun.
Stars in hats throw a glittery bash,
While meteors crash and giggle with flair.

Galaxies twirl, they know the steps,
Of a dance only the universe preps.
The black holes gossip, oh what a scene,
As they joke about their dark cuisine.

A supernova's countdown turns into cheer,
With the galaxies watching, we have no fear.
Gravity's grip can't hold us still,
Together we laugh, against cosmic will.

So let's toast to stars, and laugh out loud,
In this swirling chaos, we're the proud.
We float and we frolic, with humor that flies,
Transcending the mundane, under starry skies!

Twilight in the Milky Way

In twilight's glow, the stars conspire,
With a chuckle and a wink, they never tire.
Black holes hum to a goofy beat,
While comets waddle with silly feet.

Jupiter's storms are a wild ride,
With banded laughter swirling wide.
Saturn's rings are the cosmic bling,
As alien choirs burst out and sing.

Twilight plays with shadows so bright,
Spinning tales that twinkle at night.
In this vast expanse of cosmic glee,
Every twinkling star has a story, you see.

So let's gather 'round this celestial flare,
With laughter echoing everywhere.
In the Milky Way's embrace, we find our way,
To tickle the universe, dance and sway!

The Gravity of Forgotten Tales

In a world where pink moons wobble,
Jellyfish float in a cosmic bubble.
Rabbits play chess on a starry map,
While aliens tap dance in a solar trap.

A comet sneezes, it's quite a sight,
Knocking out planets with sheer delight.
Black holes giggle when they consume,
Lost socks and toys in an endless gloom.

Space cows munch grass on a noodle strand,
With a side of stardust, oh isn't it grand?
Galactic gossip, the stars all chat,
About life on Earth and that silly cat.

So let's toast to tales of boundless cheer,
With glasses of juice that sparkle and clear.
For gravity laughs at the silliest schemes,
In the cosmos where nothing is as it seems.

Chasing Celestial Shadows

Meteorites dance in a festive queue,
While comets wear sombreros, how 'bout you?
The Milky Way's a carnival bright,
Where showering stars take flight in the night.

Space squirrels glide on a rainbow beam,
Juggling asteroids like a cosmic dream.
Jupiter's rings are a disco ball,
While Martians do boogie, having a ball.

Pluto's a dog that chases his tail,
Around a frisbee that flies without fail.
Constellations wink with a cheeky grin,
While cosmic dust sprites sled down with a spin.

Let's chase the shadows of laughter untamed,
In the skies where no two are ever the same.
For in this wild chase, we shall find joy,
As the universe plays with its favorite toy.

Interstellar Reverie

Floating on clouds made of candy swirl,
I found a secret, this cosmic pearl.
Dancing in space with a jelly bean,
Intergalactic dreams unseen and serene.

Saturn spins like a hula hoop dare,
While Venus sings songs with a quirky flair.
Galactic rainbows paint the night sky,
While Martians sip soda and munch on pie.

A cosmic party with lights that astound,
Where black holes hide treasures profoundly bound.
Cosmic confetti falls with a pop,
As the universe giggles, not wanting to stop.

So here's to the fun in vast, swirling space,
A whimsical journey, a wild, funny chase.
In the stillness of night, where dreams often roam,
Let laughter echo as we find our way home.

Beyond the Celestial Veil

Behind a curtain of shimmering stardust,
Lies a world where giggles are a must.
Planets that bounce in a jelly-like way,
Trading their secrets at the end of the day.

A starfish spins tales about cosmic thrills,
While laughing Saturn reels from his fills.
Nebulas twirl in a glittery show,
As space whales glide happily below.

Quirky constellations tell bedtime lore,
Of adventures on planets we all adore.
Cosmic comedians take center stage,
With jokes that age better than space-age.

So let's peek beyond this celestial veil,
Where hilarity reigns on a comet's tail.
For in the laughter of endless skies,
We find the magic that never dies.

www.ingramcontent.com/pod-product-compliance
Lightning Source LLC
Chambersburg PA
CBHW071821160426
43209CB00003B/163